A souvenir guide

Morden Hall Park

London

National Trust

A green oasis in the heart of suburbia

Morden Hall Park is a vibrant example of the 'open air sitting rooms' that Octavia Hill, one of the National Trust's founders, so passionately advocated. Located in the London borough of Merton, the park offers respite from the busy suburban streets that surround it.

Amidst the bustling suburbs of south London lies the peaceful, green haven of Morden Hall Park. Home to a vast array of wildlife and a reminder of the milling industries that once lined the River Wandle, the park has been a much-loved destination for local people for the last 50 years.

A place to discover

The park has been many things throughout its colourful history: a rural marsh, home to a thriving snuff-milling industry, a landscaped deer-park and the venue for some quite extraordinary parties. Its story has been shaped as much by the River Wandle running through it as it has by the people who once lived here. Visitors who step through the gates can be forgiven for imagining themselves to be in the middle of the English countryside. Surrounded by meadows, trees and the gentle sounds of birdsong and running water, the park offers a rare sense of discovery, unlike more manicured city parks.

A precious legacy

Morden Hall Park is the legacy of Gilliat Edward Hatfeild. He was responsible for not only protecting his Morden Hall estate from the rapid urbanisation which threatened to engulf it, but also for developing strong links with the local community that continue to this day. Although Gilliat Edward Hatfeild died in 1941,

he is still remembered by local people for his unassuming generosity and gentle character.

Free for all

Unusually for a National Trust property, Morden Hall Park is open 365 days a year and has no entrance fee. When Gilliat Edward Hatfeild donated his estate to the National Trust, he stated in his will that 'a fee shall not be charged ... nor the gates kept locked ... so that my Morden estate shall be open to the public', and so it remains today.

Opposite An autumn walk in the park

Left Engaging families with Morden Hall Park

Below The River Wandle in autumn

Key dates	
Before 1536	Marsh lands owned by Abbey of Westminster
1554	Estate bought by Garth family
1750	Eastern snuff mill built
By 1770	Morden Hall built by Richard Garth V
1830	Western snuff mill built
1834	Taddy & Co. leases the snuff mills
1841	Hatfeild family in full control of snuff-milling business
1867	Gilliat Hatfeild purchases Morden Hall
1906	Gilliat Edward Hatfeild inherits estate
1941	Gilliat Edward Hatfeild dies and gives Morden Hall Park to the National Trust

The People

The early owners of Morden

Visitors to the park today would find it hard to believe that nearly 1000 years ago it was little more than boggy fields and marshes belonging to Westminster Abbey. In 1086 the manor of Mordone was recorded in the Domesday Book as having assets of three hides (about 360 acres; 145 hectares), one mill and seven ploughs. As few as fourteen people were recorded as living here. That compares with the over 100,000 people who live in the area today.

Below The Morden wetland is a reminder of the original marshes in this area

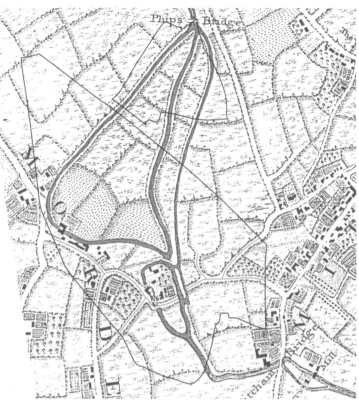

Above Gilliat Hatfeild's father, Alexander, ran the Morden snuff mill

Right The Morden estate in 1741; from John Rocque's map. Red line denotes the boundary of the present estate

Following Henry VIII's Dissolution of the Monasteries in 1536, the estate was sold to two Protestant merchants, Lionel Duckett and Edward Whitchurch, for £700. Whitchurch soon became the sole owner of the estate and in the early 1550s built a grand manor house here, which he named Growtes. Morden did not remain Whitchurch's home for long, however, and the estate changed hands again in 1553. The accession of the Catholic Queen Mary meant that wealthy Protestants like Whitchurch were in a vulnerable position, and he was compelled to put his manor up for sale.

The estate was bought by Richard Garth, a young lawyer, and remained in the Garth family for five generations. All of the subsequent four owners were also called Richard Garth. The Garths used Morden as their country retreat, away from their main home in London.

When Richard Garth V died in 1787, the estate, along with the newly built mansion of Morden Hall, passed to his three daughters: Clara, Elizabeth and Mary. They weren't interested in living in the 'wilds of Surrey', preferring fashionable London to the rural parish of Morden, so the land and buildings were leased out.

There was a succession of tenancies over the next 80 years, before Gilliat Hatfeild began buying up parts of Garth's old Morden estate. His father, Alexander, had been a partner in Taddy & Co., a firm of tobacco merchants which ran a snuff-milling industry at Morden. The Hatfeild family had proved to be astute businessmen and had married well, giving them the wealth and status to become landowners. Gilliat Hatfeild bought Morden Hall in 1867 and created a deer-park in the surrounding fields. Morden Hall Park was born.

The Hatfeilds at Morden

Far left Gilliat Hatfeild installed the clock on the tower of his new stable yard in the 1870s

Left Gilliat Edward Hatfeild (centre) in 1937

Opposite Gilliat Edward Hatfeild took particular pride in his Rose Garden

Opposite below Gilliat Edward Hatfeild preferred to live in the modest Morden Cottage

Gilliat Hatfeild was considered by some to be an eccentric. Despite his significant wealth, he chose to ignore the advances in technology of the 20th century, not allowing cars on his estate. He even refused to install electricity at Morden Hall (although there were gas lamps in the stables) and insisted on travelling to London by horse and carriage.

Hatfeild ran his estate like clockwork and was a stickler for keeping accurate time. In the 1870s he installed a clock on the top of his new stable yard, which rang every quarter hour, so that his staff would have no excuse for lateness and worked to his precise timetable.

When Hatfeild died in 1906, his son, Gilliat Edward, inherited the estate and returned from the family tobacco firm in Virginia to take up residence in Morden Hall and to run the snuff-milling business at Morden Hall Park. Like his father, he was something of a traditionalist, and was also regarded as rather unconventional in his refusal to use modern inventions.

Gilliat Edward led a modest and private life and is remembered locally for his unassuming manner and generosity. Despite inheriting a large fortune from his father, he chose to live in Morden Cottage rather than in Morden Hall,

keeping his trousers tied up with string and his watch on a bootlace.

Gilliat Edward was also a true countryman, with a great love of trees and wildlife. He stocked the river with trout for fishing, put up bird boxes on the estate and set aside an area of the park as a wildlife sanctuary.

He was extremely fond of his gardens and carried a walking stick with a tiny spade at one end, which he used to spear any stray daisies that had been left in his lawns. The Rose Garden was Gilliat Edward's particular joy and he was often seen whiling away a summer's evening deadheading his roses. His basket, secateurs and gloves were kept hidden away in a hollow tree on the lawn, waiting for him to return.

Gilliat Edward Hatfeild

Very few people can have been as generous as Gilliat Edward Hatfeild. Not only a good employer, he was a great philanthropist, and his many kindnesses are still remembered today.

By the early 20th century, snuff had become unfashionable. Later Victorians had come to consider it 'flamboyant, vulgar and offensive', and cigarette smoking had become more popular. In 1922 the workers at the Hatfeilds' tobacco company in east London went on strike in sympathy with other workers in the business, although they received better pay than most. Disappointed by the behaviour of his staff, Gilliat Edward decided to close the business, including the snuff mills at Morden

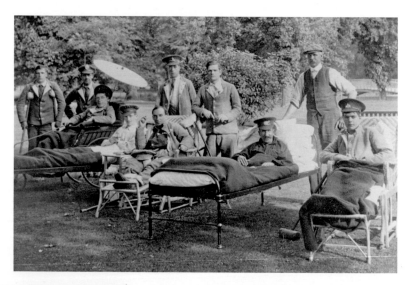

'I remember Mr Hatfeild as a tall, thin, distinguished man in a pale cream suit with a panama hat and carrying a silver walking stick with a silver handle.'

Mr Lefevre

'He was like the pied piper and wherever he went he was followed by crowds of children and he smiled and patted their heads. I have a great respect for him and all that he did.'

Eileen Spittles

Hall Park. This may sound like a harsh decision, as the Morden millers hadn't taken strike action, but he made sure that they were all given new jobs on the estate, retaining the same wages and staying in their homes. Very few tobacco merchants can be credited with being quite so generous.

It was not just in the business world that Gilliat Edward was known for his compassion; he was also a great benefactor in his personal life and shared his considerable wealth with the people around him. Morden Hall might have been too large for his own needs as a bachelor, but it wasn't left empty. It was used as a hospital at his own expense from the First World War until his death in 1941. He showed a keen interest in patients staying in the hospital, even taking those who were well enough punting on the river.

Perhaps Gilliat Edward's greatest achievement was the relationship he developed with local people. Every summer, he invited children from nearby schools to join him for a series of fabulous summer parties where they were able to enjoy his hospitality and have fun in the park.

Below Mill Cottage today

Morden Hall

Leighton & Fleet Street London

Like the park itself, Morden Hall has had a variety of roles during its lifetime. A classical mansion built between about 1750 and 1765, the external façade has changed little over the years. It is easy to imagine it as the grand country house built as the Garth family's rural retreat.

Morden Hall's life as a home covers only a short part of its history, as its owners rarely chose to live here. Richard Garth V used the hall for a little over two decades, but the later Garths preferred to enjoy the city lifestyle in London. In their absence, the hall was let out to a variety of tenants. Early residents included Thomas Sainsbury, a future Lord Mayor of London, and Sir Robert Burnett, the founder of the Vauxhall Distillery.

After half a century of domestic tenants, in the early 1830s the hall was let to William White as a 'school for young gentlemen'. Students at the school came from all over

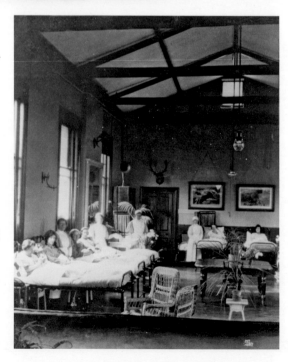

Above Morden Hall Park in the early 19th century, when it was a school. Children can be seen playing cricket on the lawn

Left The Billiard Room being used as a hospital ward

Right Patients playing cards
in the garden

the world, but the majority were from London and the local area. The school housed about 75 boys from the ages of eight to seventeen. Morden Hall was used as a school until 1867, when it was bought by Gilliat Hatfeild, who turned it back into a family home.

His son, Gilliat Edward, considered Morden Hall to be far too big for a single man and moved into Morden Cottage. However, he wanted his large house to be occupied, and so during the First World War he allowed the London Hospital to use it as a convalescent home for wounded soldiers. It must have been a pleasant and restful environment in which to recover, as photographs from the time show servicemen playing croquet and taking tea on the lawns.

After the war, Gilliat Edward used his own money to pay for the Salvation Army to continue to run it as a hospital for women and children. He became very fond of the patients and was a regular visitor.

The hall was in use as a hospital until Morden Hall Park was left to the National Trust after Gilliat Edward's death in 1941. Since then, the hall has been let out by the National Trust, bringing in a valuable income to the estate and enabling the park to continue to be run according to its donor's wishes.

'Many patients were sent from the London Hospital, Whitechapel, to Morden Hall Park, recovering from illness, needing care that was given by all at this lovely place and this was shared by Mr Hatfeild always mixing with the patients, giving lovely afternoons on the lake, rowing and punting… I suppose I was about ten at the time…the kindness surrounding all of us children, who mainly came from very poor areas of East London, was a great experience and [he] has all my gratitude.'

Marjorie Jones, née Orr

A friend of children

'We all remember the excitement of being allowed in Morden Hall for Mr Hatfeild's parties – we called him Squire Hatfeild, and how we enjoyed the boat, the donkey rides, the hoopla, other games and the special tea of sandwiches and cake in a large marquee with trestle tables. He gave us all an unforgettable day.'

It would have been extraordinary to have been a guest at one of Mr Hatfeild's tea parties. During the 1920s and 1930s, Gilliat Edward took great pleasure in inviting children from local schools to come and spend the afternoon on his estate. The park would have been alive with laughter and full of children having fun. He also sponsored Christmas parties, for which he provided all of the food and entertainment.

The parties became highlights in many of the local children's lives, as they came from very poor backgrounds and had little experience of such luxuries as cake and punting on the river. Many had moved to the area from the inner city, and considered Morden to be like the countryside.

'The sun shone always, it was such a peaceful feeling I always remember that once we were inside the grounds, it was just like being in the heart of the country. These parties were unlike anything I had ever experienced before. I was astonished that anyone should ever bother with so many hundreds of children.'

Although he was a private and unassuming gentleman, Gilliat Edward grew to have a great affinity with children that cut through class and age barriers. Whenever he appeared at the parties, the children would clamour to walk alongside him, and there are stories of him walking arm-in-arm with great lines of them.

The outbreak of the Second World War in 1939 put an end to the parties, and with Gilliat Edward's death in 1941, they never resumed.

'Mr Hatfeild always took a small group of children round his rose garden. I was chosen one year – it was wonderful. Squire Hatfeild would ask you what rose you would like and cut one for you to take home. I felt very honoured by the gesture.'

Edith Nye

Above **Bill Williams, bailiff of Morden Hall Park, with a punt full of children**

Left **Children enjoying the Morden see-saw in 1935**

'At one of the parties in the park I was one of the unfortunate ones. You used to have a mat to go down the slide, but I couldn't wait so went down without one and tore my trousers. I had to report to the headmaster the next day to say I was one of the urchins that had ripped his trousers! Mr Hatfeild stumped up to buy me a new pair! He was a wonderful, generous man, and we should not forget [him].'

Allan Vinal

Film star parties

From 1947 to 1952, Morden Hall Park hosted the most glamorous party in London – the Sunday Pictorial Film Garden Party. Each year, about 25,000 people would buy tickets to come and meet their favourite film stars, get their autographs and pay to have their photographs taken with the screen idols of the day.

A collaboration between the *Sunday Pictorial* newspaper and the British film industry, the events raised money for the NSPCC and the Church of England Children's Society. There was also a stage show with film scenes and a funfair for the excited visitors to enjoy.

For those unable to get tickets, there was the unforgettable opportunity to see the stars arrive in their Bentleys and open-top cars. Thousands of fans lined the streets outside Morden Hall Park four or five deep, all desperate for a glimpse of their idols.

'Hollywood has nothing to beat this.'
Robert Montgomery,
Once More, My Darling (1949)

Above Arm in arm: film stars enjoying the garden party

Opposite above The Morden film garden parties drew huge crowds

Opposite left Queuing for autographs

Opposite right The Italian actress Gina Lollobrigida at the 1952 film party

'Film star parties were the highlight of the year. [I] couldn't get tickets but one year I crawled in over the gate and bumped into Margaret Lockwood who shook my hand and let me carry on. I had heard of her but didn't realise how famous she was; I can't remember what she was wearing except for a large hat with feathers. Once I was in I wandered around huge crowds just to see what was happening.'

Fred Madden

'We used to stand at the gate and watch the film stars arrive. We saw a lot of stars. We used to watch the crowds going in. There was one occasion when mum allowed us to go into the park for the party. I went on a merry-go-round.'

Joy Patten

Sniffing history

Although the great waterwheels no longer turn, the two snuff mills at Morden Hall Park are a continuing reminder of the industrial heritage of the area.

The River Wandle itself was arguably the hardest worked river in the country with a great number of watermills spanning its length. Running from Croydon and Carshalton in Surrey to join the Thames at Wandsworth, the power of the fast-flowing Wandle made it an ideal milling river.

The many mills along the river produced all kinds of goods: from flour and parchment to leather and snuff. Downstream from Morden were the Merton Abbey Mills, where the Arts and Crafts designer William Morris produced his beautiful printed textiles and tapestries.

Snuff was one of the major industries that found their home along the Wandle, and the Morden mills were described as the 'elite' of the snuff mills along the river.

Left Mill Cottage and the Snuff Mill

Right The Snuff Mill today

Above Queen Charlotte was devoted to snuff; portrait by William Beechey

What is snuff?

Snuff is a finely ground tobacco product that is sniffed (and not snorted) up the nose. It was introduced to London's upper classes in around 1700 and became increasingly popular throughout the century. At the time, snuff was considered to be good for the health, boasting benefits such as improved breathing and better sight, and even providing inspiration to poets. Queen Charlotte, the wife of George III, was known as 'snuffy Charlotte' because of her love of snuff.

The first snuff mill at Morden Hall Park was built in 1750, when snuff-taking was becoming increasingly popular. It was leased in 1758 to Peter Davenport and Nathaniel Polehill, who continued the lease until 1834. At this mill, tobacco leaves were crushed into a fine powder by a series of enormous millstones, which were turned by gears and axles connected to the waterwheel.

An increasing demand for snuff led to a second mill being built about 1830. This new mill used more modern technology, having a mechanical pestle and mortar system. In their heyday, the mills would have produced about 6000 lbs of snuff each month.

Gilliat Hatfeild's grandfather, John, had married into the Taddy family, who ran a prominent snuff-making company and owned tobacco plantations in Virginia. The Hatfeild family became involved in the business, and in 1834 Taddy & Co. leased the snuff mills at Morden Hall Park, with Alexander Hatfeild (John's son) and then his son Gilliat in charge.

The Place

Gardens and landscape

We have Gilliat Hatfeild Senior to thank for putting together Morden Hall Park as we know it today. He gradually bought up pieces of land from Richard Garth's original country-house estate and the cultivated fields which surrounded it, setting himself up as a landowner of around 950 acres. This was an attempt to protect the area from the urbanisation of the early 20th century, as the village of Morden became swallowed up by the spread of south London. However, after the First World War, 800 acres of the Hatfeild estate were compulsorily purchased for new housing. The Northern Line tube was extended to Morden in the 1920s. But the core of the park survived, with Gilliat Edward working hard to protect the remainder of his estate.

The Hatfeilds' deer-park has changed very little over the years, and looks much as it would have done 150 years ago. One of the most significant additions that Hatfeild Senior made to the park was the laying-out of the

Above The avenue was planted by Gilliat Hatfeild in the late 19th century

'In the summer we used to go fruit picking with the gardeners. Us boys were sent up into the awkward places whilst the men held the ladders. Hay making was another summer activity. We like to think we were helping, throwing the straw about on the top of the cart, or riding astride the cart-horse, but I expect we were a great nuisance really.'

Eric Skelton, son of William Skelton, former gardener

Left **Mr Alderman in the Rose Garden**

Below **Mr Alderman and Mr Frankham in the Walled Garden in 1920**

Avenue – an impressive drive lined alternately with lime and horse chestnut trees. The park remained very simple in layout and design, with large lawned areas and clumps of trees. Hatfeild stocked the park with fallow deer, and cows were also kept on the estate.

Gilliat Edward maintained the park in much the same way as his father, the only major alteration being the creation of a rose garden about 1920 to the east of Morden Cottage. He was devoted to this garden, planting many different roses in an unusual irregular design of angular and circular beds – an informal style that became more common in later years.

Morden Hall Park would also have had an extensive kitchen garden, located in the area that is now the car-park. Around fourteen gardeners would have worked there, growing vegetables for the Hatfeild family, the people who lived and worked on the estate and also for patients in Morden Hall hospital. The garden had a series of large greenhouses for growing more exotic fruit and vegetables.

Local children enjoyed the opportunity to take part in some of the farming activities.

Wildlife

Morden Hall Park is not just a haven for the local people who know and love it; it is also home to a great variety of native plants, mammals, birds and insects. The diverse landscapes of the park, including meadows, grassland, marshes, waterways and woodlands, make it a valuable green space within urban London.

One of the park's landscape features is its meadows. Keen-eyed visitors may spot the remains of ridge-and-furrow ploughing, a reminder of the area's past as arable farmland. Today, the meadows feature an assortment of different grasses and wildflowers teeming with busy insects during the spring and summer.

The park is host to a great many different birds. Beside the robins, blackbirds and mallard ducks which are commonly seen in all corners of the park, it is also home to the rarely seen kingfisher, and has the heronry closest to central London. The grey herons can often be spotted standing next to the river, scanning the waters for fish. Seasonal visitors include egrets, which spend their winters in Morden. Wild parakeets are a recent addition to the park and can often be heard squawking in the trees.

The River Wandle is full of fish including roach, tench, barbel, chub and eels. Visitors have enjoyed fishing at Morden Hall Park for years, although today rights are restricted to members of the Morden Hall Fishing Club, who help to protect and maintain the park's many waterways.

A kingfisher

An orb web spider

A heron on the
Wandle weir

'I used to come tiddler catching here
just after the war. Over here was one
of our main stomping grounds. We
used to catch tiddlers with an old
sack, you could drag it along and
catch fifty to sixty in one go.'

Ken Webb

Tomorrow's Morden

The National Trust took over direct management of the park in the 1980s, respecting the spirit in which it was left and continuing to develop it as a community park, just as Gilliat Edward Hatfeild intended.

Livinggreen for the future

In 2010 work started on a groundbreaking £2.5 million project to develop a new visitor centre for the park, bringing the stable yard back into use. The Hatfeilds' Victorian stable block was renovated using sustainable building techniques and cutting-edge green technologies, opening up the heritage of the park and celebrating its relevance to local people.

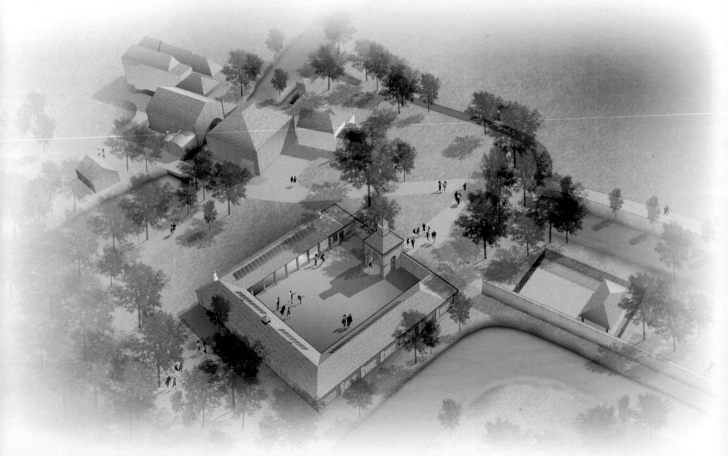

Going green

- Solar panels use the energy of the sun to produce electricity. The twelve photovoltaic panels will produce 1510 kilowatt hours (kWh) of electricity per year, and the 324 solar slates (designed to look like slate roof tiles) will produce 1325 kWh per year. Photovoltaic thermal panels use excess heat to heat water as well as generating electricity, making them doubly efficient. 22 will produce around 3400 kWh per year.

- Insulation keeps your house cool in summer and warm in winter. Sheep's wool, cork and hemp are just some of the sustainable materials used in the stable yard.

- Rainwater is collected in four giant underground tanks, each holding 3000 litres, and is used to flush the toilets.

- Air-source heat pumps extract heat from the air, and will feed into the eco underfloor heating system.

- Wood from the park fuels the wood-burning stove, heating the exhibition area and producing hot water.

- Behaviour is just as important. Staff only use electric lights when necessary, recycle as much as possible, and turn off their computers before they go home.

Above Solar slates and photovoltaic panels on the roof of the stable block provide power for the building

Opposite An artist's impression of the new visitor centre in the stable block

Right Green fingers: hands-on involvement at Morden Hall Park

Every single detail, from the three different types of hi-tech solar panels and the giant rainwater-harvesting tanks to the low-energy light bulbs and the recycled jam-jars used in vanity worktops, has been chosen carefully. It was important to select items that used as little energy during production as possible and that would be highly energy-efficient in the future.

From 2012 the weir behind the waterwheels of the snuff mills is home to a new style of turning machine: a reverse Archimedes screw turbine. This hydroelectric turbine uses the force of the water coming downstream to turn the screw and generate electricity – more than enough for the requirements of the visitor centre.

One of the National Trust's goals for the next decade is to reduce its dependence on fossil fuels and to look at new ways of harnessing renewable resources to create natural energy. Morden Hall Park is leading the way, and aims to inspire others to make changes in the way they use energy in their own homes.

The stable yard opened to the public in November 2011 and is one of the most energy-efficient historic buildings in the whole country.

The park at the heart of the local community

'I love this place. It's somewhere beautiful on the edge of London. It hasn't been mucked about with. It feels like it's my park.'

Fred Madden

When Gilliat Edward Hatfeild left his much-loved park to the National Trust in 1941, he was ensuring that it would be kept forever as a resource for the local people. Hatfeild's legacy lives on in the families, dog-walkers, joggers, cyclists and local residents who visit and enjoy it every day.

With the sustainably regenerated stable yard providing a new focus, Morden Hall Park is now a green oasis in more ways than one. Visitors not only experience a taste of the countryside in the London suburbs, they can also understand how to live greener lives themselves, while at the same time looking after our world for the generations to come.

Morden Hall Park may not boast extravagant art collections, flamboyant aristocratic families or tales of scandalous adventure, but it is incredibly important to the people living around it – the park really is at the heart of the local community.

Above Jogging in the park